THE GAME
The Greatest Rivalry in Sports

UNIVERSITY OF MICHIGAN
WOLVERINES
and
THE OHIO STATE UNIVERSITY
BUCKEYES

300 Football Trivia Q&A
and THE GAME Numerology

By Mike McGuire

ALSO BY MIKE McGUIRE

1001 U.S. Geography Trivia Q & A

500 Ohio State Football Trivia Q & A

800 Ohio State Football Trivia Q & A

1220 Ohio State Football Trivia Q & A

500 Heisman Football Trivia Q & A

The Majors Golf Trivia Q & A

Shotguns + Clay Target Sports Trivia Q & A

"The Game" Ohio State vs. Michigan 300 Football Trivia Q & A

Notre Dame "Fighting Irish" 500 Football Trivia Q & A

Michigan "Wolverine" 500 Football Trivia Q & A

COMING SOON!

Shooting Clay Target Sports Trivia Q & A

Alabama "Crimson Tide" Football Q & A

Sports Venue Trivia Q & A

Ohio Born Football Coaches Trivia Q & A

Southern Cal "Trojans" Football Q & A

THE GAME
The Greatest Rivalry in Sports

UNIVERSITY OF MICHIGAN
WOLVERINES
and
THE OHIO STATE UNIVERSITY
BUCKEYES

300 Football Trivia Q&A
and THE GAME Numerology

By Mike McGuire

member of
The National Football Foundation & College Football Hall of Fame
Football Writers Association
Intercollegiate Football Researchers Association

Additional copies available at leading bookstores
and college spirit stores throughout America.

Comments, questions, updates or additional trivia?
Contact the author

Mike McGuire
11305 E. Monument Drive
Scottsdale, AZ 85262-4746

480.488.3247 fax
mmcguire@mcguireusa.com

THE GAME
The Greatest Rivalry in Sports

UNIVERSITY OF MICHIGAN
WOLVERINES
and
THE OHIO STATE UNIVERSITY
BUCKEYES

300 Football Trivia Q&A
and THE GAME Numerology

By Mike McGuire

978-0-9772661-1-1

FIRST EDITION

Published by Mike McGuire

Order copies from
Mike McGuire
11305 E. Monument Drive
Scottsdale, AZ 85262-4746
480.563.1424

Printed in the United States of America

DEDICATION

This trivia book is dedicated to the memory of my good ol' buddy Dr. Nick Marzella of Columbus, Ohio. Nick and I played a lot of golf together, played cards until the cows came home, and always liked to dine at the newest or "hottest" restaurants in Columbus or Scottsdale. Nick would drink his favorite wine, Silver Oak, while I sipped a single malt scotch. Our conversations always came around to Ohio State football, no matter what time of the year it was. Nick loved Ohio State football like no one can describe, and he was just a true Buckeye fan! Nick was always aware of the latest news and activities surrounding the Buckeye football program. It was always a lot of fun just talking (or should I say listening) about Ohio State football with Nick!

The last picture I have of Nick is out in front of the BCS National Championship game at the AT&T Stadium in Arlington, Texas, on January 12, 2015. He is with his son-in-law Aaron Spiess, his brother Richie, and Richie's son Daniel. Nick is wearing his favorite gray Ohio State sweater with a scarlet Block "O." I am so glad he had the opportunity to be there to cheer on the Buckeyes, which helped bring home the "bacon," the National Championship, to where it belongs: Columbus, Ohio.

It's a simple phrase spoken by every Ohio State fan, but I'll miss hearing it specifically from Nick. Whenever we parted or finished up a phone conversation, Nick's last words to me were always the same: "Go Bucks!"

Magoo

PREFACE

"The Game" 300 Football Trivia Q&A was a lot of fun to write because of the tremendous amount of material available about the history, the tradition, and the competitive spirit of athletic competition between The Ohio State University Buckeyes and the University of Michigan Wolverines. "The Game," as it is widely known, is recognized as the greatest rivalry in all of sports, without question. The Ohio State/Michigan rivalry is very special! Fielding H. Yost and Francis Schmidt made it Great, Woody and Bo made it the Best, Jim Tressel made it even Better, and Urban Meyer and Jim Harbaugh will make it even Greater in the coming years! From 1935 to the present day, it has always been the last game of the regular season, with usually a lot on the line for championships, bowl games and national ranking.

All 300 questions and answers touch on "The Game." They cover the players, the coaches, the stadiums, the key plays, the bowl games, the bands, the fans, the Heisman Trophy winners and a whole lot more "nickel trivia facts." My trivia questions are meant to be fun, tricky, thought-provoking and confusing—to bring back good ol' memories while testing your knowledge of this, the greatest college football rivalry game. Laugh, cry, argue—but most of all, have fun with the trivia.

Another feature in the book is a unique "Weather Forecast" that gives GPS coordinates for each of the stadiums. The forecast will provide very accurate information to help you determine how to dress for the game and/or maybe even help you decide how to place a bet on "The Game."

The Complete Numerology Guide is a first for another way to look at "The Game." I took a little bit of author's privilege to include some century numbers by adding them in front of some of the numbers to indicate the year of "The Game" or the year that the question refers to. I think you will enjoy the additional trivia information.

Yes, I am a little biased in this book (but that is OK!) because I've been following the Ohio State Buckeyes since 1954, when I was seven years old. I was well indoctrinated into becoming a true Buckeye fan watching Heisman Trophy winner Howard "Hopalong" Cassady in 1955 and the blocking of Jim Parker, who was an Outland Trophy winner, All-American, and future All-Pro Player and inductee into the College and the Pro Football halls of fame. Since I became a Buckeye fan, we've had National Championships in 1954, 1957 and 1961 under Woody Hayes, the "Super Sophs" of 1968, The National Championship Team for Jim Tressel in 2002 and another one for Urban Meyer in 2014. It has been a great run, and I look forward to even more exciting games and great players in the future, continuing to solidify "The Game" as the greatest rivalry in all of sports.

Mike McGuire
Go Bucks! BEAT MICHIGAN!

HOW TO USE "THE GAME" FOOTBALL TRIVIA Q&A

I offer the following suggestions to increase your enjoyment of this trivia book, which is meant to be fun and to enhance the understanding of the "greatest rivalry in all of college football."

This book is great to use as a "party starter" for any Buckeye or Wolverine gathering, before kick-off, and is an excellent way to meet new fans while learning about the great traditions, history and records of "The Game." The book is laid out in a format of 20 questions and answers so users can go along at their own pace. You can use the book to host a trivia contest where each question is worth 5 points, and then you can award prizes to individuals or teams for their skill and knowledge of "The Game."

Tailgating ... A great way to pass the time as the hamburgers and hotdogs are cooking on the grill. Play to see who cooks or who cleans up after the meal!

On the road ... Driving to and from "The Game," trivia can help make the miles pass faster. Play to see who drives and who asks the questions, or who buys the next tank of gas, food or cocktails.

On an airplane, bus, subway or train ... A good way to study and improve your knowledge of "The Game," the traditions, history, records, players, coaches and more. Upon your arrival, impress your friends with your knowledge of "The Game." Maybe even meet other fans who are traveling to "The Game."

Local pub or pizza joint ... Pizza and beer always taste better with great sports trivia conversations, discussions and arguments, and it doesn't get any better than "The Game."

As a gift ... The book is always a wonderful gift for any great Buckeye or Wolverine fan and one that will be valued and remembered for years to come.

First date going to "The Game" ... A great conversation starter if you have prior knowledge that your date is a football fan!

In the bathroom ... OK! But please keep the book on your nightstand or bookshelf.

Note: Use "The Game" Weather Forecast feature for the latest weather before, during and after "The Game." Handy reference material, facts and figures are contained in the Numerology of *"The Game" 300 Football Trivia Q&A* feature to just have a lot more fun.

Share the unique ways you have used *"The Game" 300 Football Trivia Q&A* book by writing to:

Mike McGuire
11305 E. Monument Dr.
Scottsdale, Arizona 85262-4746

TABLE OF CONTENTS

 GROUP **1** QUESTIONS

1-1 "Those fellows put their pants on one leg at a time, the same as everyone" is a cliché attributed to which Ohio State Head Football Coach?

1-2 "Bo" Schembechler beat Woody Hayes three years in a row once. What were the three years?

1-3 **T or F:** Ohio State was the first team since Minnesota in 1933-35 to go undefeated in three consecutive seasons.

1-4 What are the official mascots of the Ohio State Buckeyes and the Michigan Wolverines?

1-5 **T or F:** Coach Bo Schembechler was an assistant coach to Woody Hayes during two different periods.

1-6 Which game do historians state truly foreshadows the future of the "Greatest Rivalry" in sports?

1-7 What was the difference in the famous "Snow Bowl" in 1950 that helped Michigan win a major upset?

1-8 What is the only Big Ten team Ohio State does not have an all-time winning percentage record against, including the University of Chicago?

1-9 In 28 seasons, Woody Hayes won five National Championships. In 21 seasons, how many did Bo Schembechler win?

1-10 **T or F:** Ohio State led the Big Ten in 1950 and was granted the option of cancelling the now famous "Snow Bowl" because of the blizzard in Columbus, Ohio. Ohio State refused to cancel.

1-11 How many National Championships did Fielding H. Yost win in 25 seasons at Michigan?

1-12 Who led Michigan to beat Ohio State 18-0 in Columbus in a game titled "Climax of the Wolverines," returning as a major gridiron power?

1-13 How many years did Bo Schembechler coach after Woody's dismissal?

1-14 What was Lloyd Carr's record against Top-Ten ranked teams?

1-15 What four Michigan players have won the Chic Harley Award presented by The Touchdown Club of Columbus?

1-16 What was "The 10-Year War?"

1-17 How many Big Ten Championships did Coach Woody Hayes win?

1-18 How many times has the rivalry been the "de facto" Big Ten Championship Game?

1-19 Who is the only Ohio State Head Football Coach to dot the "i" in Script Ohio?

1-20 Which former Wolverine QB has thrown a touchdown pass in Super Bowls #38 & #39, and to which former Ohio State defensive player?

GROUP **1** ANSWERS

1-1 Francis Schmidt in 1929, before beating Michigan four years (1934-1937) in a row! Now known as the "Gold Pants Award."

1-2 1976, 1977, 1978. Twice in Columbus and once in Ann Arbor.

1-3 True, after beating Michigan in 2014. (Might extend the record in 2015.)

1-4 "Brutus Buckeye," and Michigan does not have a mascot!

1-5 True: 1952-1953 (Graduate Assistant) and 1959-1963 (Assistant)

1-6 1926. Michigan (#17) upset undefeated Ohio State (#16). Both teams finished 7-1, but this game cost Ohio State a Conference Title.

1-7 A blocked punt, recovered by Michigan with 47 seconds left in the first half, making the score 9-3.

1-8 The University of Michigan Wolverines, Ann Arbor, Michigan

1-9 None. Zip!

1-10 True. Class act by Coach Wes Fesler. Ohio State lost 9-3. Michigan won the Title and a Rose Bowl trip.

1-11 Six National Championships and 10 Big Ten Conference Titles.

1-12 "Old 98" Tom Harmon in 1938, going on to win the Heisman Trophy in 1940

1-13 11 years, for a total of 21

1-14 19-8, overall record at Michigan 122-40

1-15 Bob Timberlake (1964), Jim Harbaugh (1986), Desmond Howard (1991), Charles Woodson (1997). Ohio State players have won six awards.

1-16 Woody Hayes vs. Bo Schembechler (1969-1979)

1-17 13. Bo also won 13

1-18 22 times, with "The Game" affecting the determination of the championship an additional 27 times.

1-19 Wayne Woodrow "Woody" Hayes, Head Coach 1951-1978

1-20 Quarterback Tom Brady to Linebacker Mike Vrabel

 GROUP **2** QUESTIONS

2-1   "Senior Tackle" was started in 1913 by which Head Football Coach?

2-2   **T or F:** All five games played in Ann Arbor, Michigan during the "10-Year War" were played in front of 103,000-plus fans.

2-3   What was Bo Schembechler's real legal name?

2-4   Ohio State took the following records: 9-0-1 in 1993, 11-0 in 1995, and 10-0 in 1996, going into "The Game," and what happened?

2-5   In an unprecedented display of sportsmanship and appreciation, Ohio State fans gave which Michigan player a standing ovation at the game's end?

2-6   Ohio State won its first National Championship in which year, under which Head Coach?

2-7   Which three Wolverine Head Coaches defeated Ohio State in each of their first three games?

2-8   Who was the first high school athlete to have his picture on a box of Wheaties?

2-9   What was Fielding H. Yost's record for consecutive wins against the Ohio State Buckeyes?

2-10 What famous humorist, cartoonist and OSU Alum designed the cover of the 1936 Ohio State–Michigan football program?

2-11 Head Football Coach Woody Hayes referred to Michigan as what?

2-12 Between 1984 and 2006, how many outright Big Ten Championships did Ohio State win?

2-13 After the renovation of Ohio Stadium (now with 104,944 seats), where does it rank in capacity compared to other college football stadiums?

2-14 When was the last time "Standing-Room Only" tickets were sold for a game in the Ohio State Buckeyes Stadium?

2-15 Going into "The Game" in 2006, what was the series record for the last 50 years?

2-16 What state has the most native sons to win a Heisman Trophy?

2-17 Which year did Ohio State stop Michigan on four attempts to score inside the four-yard line, then drive 99-1/2 yards to take the lead and win the Big Ten Championship undefeated?

2-18 Which year was the first time the Buckeyes and the Wolverines entered into "The Game" with undefeated teams?

2-19 Between 1937 and 1957, how many times did Michigan lose to the Buckeyes in Ann Arbor, Michigan?

2-20 The 81 combined points in "The Game" of 2006 was the most since which game?

GROUP 2 ANSWERS

2-1　John Wilce. Now it's always held during the last practice before "The Game" in "The Shoe."

2-2　True! When played in Columbus, the crowd was 87,000-88,000 each year of the five games.

2-3　Glenn Edward "Bo" Schembechler, Jr. "Bo" came from his sister, who had trouble saying "brother."

2-4　The Ohio States Buckeyes lost each year! OUCH!

2-5　Tom Harmon, 1940. No other Wolverine has ever been so honored before or since.

2-6　1942, Paul Brown

2-7　Fielding H. Yost, Fritz Crisler and Lloyd Carr

2-8　Chris Spielman, 1983. Two-time All-American at Ohio State, 1986-1987.

2-9　Nine years (1901-1909). Jim Tressel (OSU) had seven wins in a row through 2010.

2-10　James Thurber. Also, famous cartoonist Milton Caniff (Terry & the Pirates) designed covers for Ohio State football programs.

2-11　"That State Up North" or "That Team Up North." He never said the word "Michigan."

2-12　None

2-13　Fourth. Michigan is first with 109,901. Penn State is second with 107,282. Texas A&M is third with 106,512.

2-14　1925, for the Michigan game

2-15　24-24-2

2-16　The Great Buckeye State: OHIO

2-17　1954

2-18　1970. It was an Ohio State victory, 20-9.

2-19　Once in 1955; the Buckeyes won 31-14. Woody's first victory in Ann Arbor.

2-20　1902. Michigan won 86-0.

GROUP 3 QUESTIONS

3-1   Which Head Coach pledged that his players will "most especially make the school proud in 310 days in Ann Arbor"?

3-2   In 2006, Michigan led the nation in rushing defense at 29.9 yards. How many yards did the Buckeyes rush against them in their 42-39 victory?

3-3   Vic Janowicz punted how many times and for how many yards in the 1950 "Snow Bowl" game?

3-4   Which years did new (2015) Head Coach Jim Harbaugh play QB for "Bo" and the Michigan Wolverines?

3-5   Who said: "If he weren't from Michigan, I'd like to have my own son play for him."?

3-6   **T or F:** Only five of 21 Ohio State Head Football Coaches have a winning record against Michigan.

3-7   Which Head Buckeye Coach started the tradition "Countdown" Pep Rally during Michigan Week?

3-8   Which Athletic Director at Ohio State played halfback and QB at Michigan?

3-9   Before Woody won (17-0) at Ann Arbor in 1955, how many seasons had it been since the last victory for the Buckeyes in Michigan Stadium?

3-10 **T or F:** Upon its completion in 1922, Ohio Stadium was the largest poured concrete structure in the world.

3-11 How many unbeaten seasons have been destroyed in the past Ohio State-Michigan games through 2014?

3-12 **T or F:** In 1946, with Michigan leading 55-0, they kicked a field goal late in the game.

3-13 In Woody's first 18 seasons, how many times did Michigan win the Big Ten Title?

3-14 What year was the first game with Michigan where the winner would be the outright Big Ten Champion?

3-15 Which three years have Ohio State vs. Michigan both been undefeated-untied since 1935?

3-16 Who holds the record for the most interceptions in "The Game" as a Buckeye?

3-17 **T or F:** "The Best Damn Band in the Land" performed at half-time during the "Snow Bowl" game against Michigan in 1950.

3-18 How do Meeechegan™ fans spell Columbus, Ohio?

3-19 How many Ohio State Head Football Coaches did not BEAT Michigan in their career?

3-20 Which two FBs wore/used the same chin strap in "The Game" seven years apart?

 GROUP 3 ANSWERS

3-1 Jim Tressel, and they did. Tressel won his first Michigan game in Ann Arbor 2001.

3-2 187 yards, and they threw for four touchdowns

3-3 21 punts, for 685 yards, a 33-yard average

3-4 1983-1986. He started in 1984 until an injury sidelined him, but started in 1985-1986.

3-5 Woody Hayes, in regards to Michigan Head Coach Bennie Oosterbaan.

3-6 True: Francis Schmidt, Woody Hayes, Earle Bruce, Jim Tressel & Urban Meyer

3-7 John Wilce in 1919, when Chic Harley handily won "The Game"

3-8 Rick Bay, 1961-1964. He did not earn a letter, OSU AD 1984-1987.

3-9 18 years (1937 by Francis Schmidt)

3-10 True; it's now on the U.S. National Register of Historic Places

3-11 10

3-12 True. Woody returned the favor in 1968, going for two points and winning 50-14.

3-13 One time in 1964

3-14 1944. Ohio State 19, Michigan 14. Heisman Trophy winner Les Horvath scored the winning touchdown.

3-15 1970, 1973 and 2006

3-16 "Chic" Harley against Michigan, with four in 1919

3-17 True. The now-famous photo shows the band doing the Hula Dance formation.

3-18 Cowlumbus, Ahia

3-19 10 coaches; 1897-1912 and 1946-1950

3-20 Fullback Bob Ferguson (1961) and Fullback Jim Otis (1968); each scored four touchdowns.

GROUP 4 QUESTIONS

4-1 **T or F:** During the "10-Year War," Ohio State and the U of M split 10 Big Ten Conference Titles and had eight second finishes.

4-2 What year was the inaugural game for the "Greatest Rivalry" in college football?

4-3 What was Michigan Head Football Coach Fielding H. Yost's nickname?

4-4 Who holds the record for the most rushing yards against Michigan in "The Game?"

4-5 What was Head Football Coach Bo Schembechler's record at Michigan?

4-6 Which Michigan Head Football Coach, during his collegiate career, was a Big Ten Baseball Batting Champion, Scoring Champion in Basketball and Big Ten Touchdown Leader?

4-7 Which three Ohio State coaches have had a 2-0 winning record against Michigan?

4-8 **T or F:** Michigan played in the very first Rose Bowl Game.

4-9 Between 1970 through 1975, Michigan entered "The Game" without a loss every year. What was their win/loss record afterwards?

4-10 Woody Hayes won how many Big Ten Championships, National Championships and Rose Bowls?

4-11 **T or F:** Unranked Michigan beat 9th-ranked Florida in the Capital One Bowl in Lloyd Carr's final game, beating the future Ohio State Coach Urban Meyer and his Heisman Trophy winner, Tim Tebow.

4-12 Who was the first Michigan coach to go 0-2 against the Buckeyes?

4-13 Although more than 100,000 people have probably said they were at the "Snow Bowl" Game, what is the published attendance number?

4-14 How many years had it been since both OSU and U of M were undefeated before the 2006 game?

4-15 After the 1969 upset loss to Michigan, a custom-made rug was located outside the locker room by Head Coach Woody Hayes that stated what?

4-16 What was called "one of the greatest feats in American sports?"

4-17 Because of the No-Repeat Rule, who went to the Rose Bowl in 1955 after Ohio State BEAT Michigan for the Big Ten Championship?

4-18 What was Michigan's record against Ohio State through 1927 when they opened Michigan Stadium?

4-19 How many times did Archie Griffin score in his four games against the Michigan Wolverines?

4-20 In the "Ten-Year War," was Ohio State ever not ranked?

GROUP 4 ANSWERS

4-1   True! 5 and 5

4-2   1897. Michigan won 34–0. It was Michigan's 18th year of football, seventh for Ohio State.

4-3   "Hurry-up"

4-4   Chris "Beanie" Wells in 2007, at 222 yards

4-5   194-48-5, winning or sharing 13 Big Ten Titles; career record 234-65-8 (40-17-3) at Miami University (MAC League 1963-1968)

4-6   Bennie Oosterbaan, one of the greatest athletes in history!

4-7   Francis Schmidt, Jim Tressel and Urban Meyer

4-8   True, beating Stanford 49-0 in 1902.

4-9   Michigan lost in 1970, 1972, 1974 & 1975, won in 1971 and tied in 1973.

4-10   13 Big Ten Championships, five National Championships, and was four out of eight in the Rose Bowl.

4-11   True! In 2008, Michigan won that game 41-35.

4-12   Rich Rodriquez, 2008-2009, actually 0-3(losing in 2010). Record was 15-22, worst record of any Head Coach in Michigan history. Watch what he is doing at Arizona.

4-13   50,503, in a blizzard

4-14   33 years, 1973

4-15   1969: Michigan 24, Ohio State 12; 1970: Michigan 9, Ohio State 20. It Worked!

4-16   Vic Janowicz's 21-yard field goal in the "Snow Bowl" game, 1950

4-17   The Michigan State Spartans

4-18   19-3-2, and they beat Ohio State 21-0

4-19   One game, 1972, which Ohio State won 14-11

4-20   Yes! 1971

 GROUP 5 QUESTIONS

5-1 Michigan lost the 1974 game 12-10 because which Ohio State kicker hit four field goals?

5-2 What is the greatest margin of victory by either Ohio State or Michigan in "The Game?"

5-3 Which Buckeye victory stopped the 21-game Michigan winning streak?

5-4 Woody Hayes favored the running game over passing for many seasons. What nickname did he earn in regards to his running game?

5-5 **T or F:** Ohio State is the only school to perform "Script Ohio."

5-6 When did Ohio State meet Michigan for the first time with the Big Ten Title on the line?

5-7 What was Head Coach John Cooper's record against the Michigan Wolverines?

5-8 What years did Ohio State and Michigan join the Big Ten Conference?

5-9 What is the longest run from scrimmage against Michigan by a Buckeye?

5-10 Which Michigan QB has attempted the most passes against Ohio State?

5-11 Who was Bo Schembechler's college football coach?

5-12 Between 1968 and 2008 (40 seasons), what was the biggest margin of victory?

5-13 Who was the first Michigan coach to win four straight bowl games?

5-14 Who is the only Buckeye hero of the Michigan game who has had a ticker tape parade in Columbus, Ohio?

5-15 What buildings are normally called "The Big House," which is the nickname of the Michigan Stadium?

5-16 Which Wolverine player closed out his career at Ohio State with two rushing TDs, two passing TDs, returned an interception for a TD and converted on four extra points?

5-17 What corporation wanted to buy the rights and rename "The Game" for a million dollars in 2004?

5-18 How many interceptions did Michigan have against Rex Kern in the 1969 "upset loss?"

5-19 Which stadium held the 100th meeting of "The Game?"

5-20 What year did Ohio State and Michigan play their first Big Ten Conference game?

GROUP 5 ANSWERS

5-1   Tom Klaban

5-2   Michigan (86), Ohio State (0): 1902, 15 TDs, 1 PATs. Game was shortened by 10 minutes.

5-3   1972, Ohio State (14), Michigan (11) with two great goal-line stands

5-4   "Three Yards and a Cloud of Dust"

5-5   False. Michigan did it first, Stanford tried it and misspelled Ohio.

5-6   1944. Ohio State (18), Michigan (14)

5-7   Two wins, 10 losses and a tie

5-8   Ohio State in 1913; Michigan returned in 1917, after leaving in 1906. Big Ten Conference play started in 1896.

5-9   Dan "Boom" Herron, 89 yards, 2010 game

5-10   Tom Brady, 56 in 1998

5-11   Woody Hayes at Miami University 1949-1950. "Bo" was a tackle.

5-12   35 points in 2008 and 36 points in 1968

5-13   Lloyd Carr. 2001 Citrus Bowl, 2000 Orange Bowl, 1999 Citrus Bowl, and 1998 Rose Bowl. Later lost four Bowl Games in a row.

5-14   Chic Harley, upon his return for the Homecoming Game in 1948, 29 years after his final game.

5-15   Maximum Security Federal Prisons, e.g. Alcatraz in San Francisco Bay

5-16   Tom Harmon, 1940, winning 40-0

5-17   SBC; the offer was declined.

5-18   Four by Rex Kern and two more by a sub, for a total of six

5-19   Michigan Stadium, November 22, 2003. Odd years at Michigan, even numbered years at Ohio State. Michigan won 35-31.

5-20   1918. It took 16 tries for Ohio State to win for the first time, 13-3 at Ann Arbor on October 25, 1919.

 GROUP **6** QUESTIONS

6-1 Ohio State played in four Rose Bowls in a row, with three wins and a tie. Which four years?

6-2 Name the two highest-scoring coaches, one each, from Ohio State and Michigan.

6-3 Which Ohio State Coach broke the string known as the "Graveyard of Coaches?"

6-4 **T or F:** In 1975, the Buckeyes scored twice on Michigan in the last two minutes to pull out a 21-14 victory and held on to the #1 ranking, then were upset by UCLA in the Rose Bowl to lose another National Championship.

6-5 What did Francis Schmidt teams do the first four years against Michigan?

6-6 **T or F:** Bo's Michigan teams always finished ranked except once in 21 seasons and were in the final Top Ten 16 seasons in both major polls.

6-7 Next to Bo Schembechler's overall record of 198-48-5, who is second in overall wins?

6-8 Which seasons apply to Fielding H. Yost's teams nicknamed "Point-A-Minute," outscoring their opponents 2,821 to 42?

6-9 Which team was known as the "Super Sophomores!"?

6-10 Michigan Heisman Trophy Winner Tom Harmon strongly supported which Buckeye to win the Heisman Trophy?

6-11 Who blocked Vic Janowicz's punt with 47 seconds left in the first half of the "Snow Bowl?"

6-12 **T or F:** In 1929, Knute Rockne wanted to be the new Head Coach at Ohio State after 11 years at Notre Dame so he could coach against Michigan in the Big Ten Conference.

6-13 Who is the only running back to lead the Big Ten in rushing for three straight years?

6-14 **T or F:** Michigan Stadium was designed after the Yale Bowl and today is the largest stadium in the United States at its official capacity of 109,901.

6-15 What was Brady Hoke's four-year record?

6-16 Which Michigan player "flaunted" the Heisman Trophy pose in "The Game?"

6-17 **T or F:** Ohio State and Michigan first met in 1897 and have met every year since 1918.

6-18 How many of Head Coach Woody Hayes' teams shutout the Michigan Wolverines?

6-19 How many ties have the Ohio State Buckeyes and the Michigan Wolverines had over the years?

6-20 What does TBDBITL stand for?

 GROUP 6 ANSWERS

6-1   1972, 1973 (tied 10-10), 1974, 1975

6-2   Francis Schmidt "Close the Gates of Mercy"; Fielding H. Yost "Point-a-Minute"

6-3   Woody Hayes upon being hired in 1951 (previously five coaches in 11 seasons)

6-4   True. Ohio State had beaten UCLA earlier in the season. This was UCLA Coach Dick Vermel's only Rose Bowl Game.

6-5   They won all four by shutouts!

6-6   True! A great record!

6-7   Fielding H. Yost with 165-29-10; Lloyd Carr is third with a record of 121-40-0.

6-8   1901-1905, 56 straight wins!

6-9   1968 National Champions, The Ohio State University Buckeyes

6-10 Howard "Hopalong" Cassady after the 1954 Michigan game, a 21-7 victory for Ohio State

6-11 Tony Momsen. Then he fell on the ball in the end zone to score the winning points. Half-time score was 9-3, and this was the final score, as neither team scored in the second half.

6-12 True, but the Notre Dame powers that be convinced Knute Rockne to stay at Notre Dame. Google "Blue-Gray Sky" for some more history.

6-13 Archie Griffin, two-time Heisman Trophy winner, 1973-1975

6-14 True. Since November 8, 1975, Michigan has drawn a crowd in excess of 100,000 for more than 200 games straight!

6-15 31-20, 18-14 in Big Ten play, and 1-3 against Ohio State

6-16 Desmond Howard in the 1991 game, following a 93-yard punt return for a touchdown!

6-17 True

6-18 Three: 1955, 1960 and 1962

6-19 Six: 1900, 1910, 1941, 1949, 1973 and 1992

6-20 "The Best Damn Band in the Land" — The Ohio State University Marching Band of 192 marching members.

 GROUP **7** QUESTIONS

7-1   When was the only time in Woody's first 18 seasons that Michigan won its only Big Ten Championship?

7-2   What year did the Buckeyes outscore their opponents 40.2 to 7.8 PPG, and no other team came within four touchdowns of Ohio State, going into "The Game?"

7-3   Which Buckeye Head Coach won four Big Ten Titles, a Cotton Bowl, a Fiesta Bowl and was 5-4 against the Michigan Wolverines?

7-4   **T or F:** Ohio State led the nation in attendance in 2014 after "The Game" for the first time since 1973.

7-5   Which Ohio State Head Coach has a double-digit winning record in "The Game?"

7-6   Who stated: "Football builds character."?

7-7   Which player, who played in three of "The Games," led the country two consecutive years in scoring, which remains unmatched to this day?

7-8   What was Jim Tressel's Bowl Championship Series (BCS) record?

7-9   How many undefeated seasons did Woody Hayes have in his 28-year career at Ohio State?

7-10   Archie Griffin, the only two-time Heisman Trophy winner, ran for 100-plus yards in how many consecutive games?

7-11   **T or F:** Urban Meyer, Nick Saban, Jim Tressel, Mark Dantonio and Pete Carroll were all assistant coaches under Earle Bruce at Ohio State.

7-12   Yankee Stadium is "The House Ruth Built." What is "The House that Harley Built?"

7-13   Which two Ohio State Heisman Trophy winners made "famous fumbles" early in their collegiate careers?

7-14   "Hey Jude," by The Beatles, spent the longest time on the charts the same year Ohio State was #1 and won a National Championship. What year was it?

7-15   **T or F:** Michigan beat Ohio State in each of the teams' stadium dedication games in 1922 (Ohio Stadium) and 1927 (Michigan Stadium).

7-16   Who said the following: "The thing I'm most proud of about my college career is that I played on four teams that never lost to Michigan."

7-17   What year did Title IX legislation allow women to join the Ohio State Marching Band?

7-18   Who stated: "There is nothing that beats when the Ohio State Marching Band and the sousaphone player dots the "i" for Script Ohio."?

7-19   **T or F:** Woody Hayes won eight out of 10 Michigan Games from 1954 until 1964.

7-20   Ohio State's 1975 win at Michigan (21-14) stopped Michigan's consecutive home win record at what number?

GROUP 7 ANSWERS

7-1   1964: Michigan (10), Ohio State (0)

7-2   1969: Then Ohio State lost 24-12!

7-3   Earle Bruce, 1979-1987

7-4   True! Averaged 106,000-plus fans per game.

7-5   Woody Hayes: 16-11-1 vs. BO at 4-5-1

7-6   Fielding H. Yost, promoting the concept of "Student-Athletes" at the time

7-7   #98 Tom Harmon, 1939 & 1940

7-8   Won 5 out of 8, with a National Championship in 2002

7-9   Four: 1954, 1961, 1968 & 1973; 1954 & 1968 Perfect Seasons

7-10 31 straight games between 1971-1973

7-11 True. Earle Bruce always had a great group of assistant coaches.

7-12 Ohio Stadium. "The Horseshoe." "The Shoe." 1922.

7-13 Archie Griffin in his first game in 1972; Eddie George's two fumbles against Illinois 1992

7-14 1968

7-15 True: 19-0 in Ohio Stadium in 1922 and 21-0 in Michigan Stadium in 1927. WOW!
      Two shutouts for Michigan in stadium dedication games!

7-16 #45 Archie Griffin

7-17 1972, federal law. In 1973, women joined the band and now represent approx. 20-25%.

7-18 Sportscaster Beano Cook

7-19 True: only losses in 1956 and 1959

7-20 41 games

GROUP 8 QUESTIONS

8-1 What game, called "The Upset of the Century," was Ohio State's most costly defeat?

8-2 **T or F:** Jesse Owens was a wide receiver for Francis Schmidt during the season he also won four Gold Medals in the 1936 Berlin Olympic Games and helped to BEAT Michigan.

8-3 Ohio State's first victory against the Wolverines was highlighted by which three-time All-American?

8-4 Who kicked a 56-yard field goal to beat Ohio State 34-31 in 1988?

8-5 How many times between 1970 and 1975 were Ohio State and Michigan ranked in the Top Five of the AP Poll before their game?

8-6 Describe the "Mirror Lake Jump."

8-7 Which Wolverine Head Football Coach brought the famous Winged Helmet to Michigan?

8-8 **T or F:** Lloyd Carr had a winning record for Michigan against two of their three rivals.

8-9 Who stated this about Michigan Stadium: "The hole that Yost dug, Crisler paid for, Canham carpeted and Schembechler fills every cotton-pickin' Saturday afternoon."?

8-10 Who came through unblocked to block a Michigan punt in the fourth quarter, after which the ball was picked up by Todd Bell, who ran it in for the game-winning touchdown?

8-11 When did the Ohio State goal posts get torn down for the very first time?

8-12 Which Head Football Coach passed away on the eve of the historic #1 OSU vs. #2 U of M game?

8-13 Through 2006, what is the combined win/loss record vs. Michigan for coaches Bruce, Cooper and Tressel?

8-14 Who was the first Head Football Coach to BEAT Michigan in 1919?

8-15 What two brothers from Akron, Ohio, played against each other in "The Game" in 1957?

8-16 **T or F:** It has been written that Michigan used "Tramp" players in the 1890s to win several games for Coach Fielding H. Yost.

8-17 Who holds the record for the most PATs by a Buckeye against the Michigan Wolverines?

8-18 What happened to the Buckeyes and the Wolverines the week before the 2007 game?

8-19 **T or F:** For each of the five seasons between 1972-1976, either Bo or Woody won the Big Ten Coach of the Year award.

8-20 What was Michigan Head Coach Lloyd Carr's record against the Ohio State Buckeyes?

 GROUP 8 ANSWERS

8-1 1969. U of M 24–OSU 12. Ohio State was undefeated and a 17-point favorite.

8-2 False. There were no Wide Receivers in 1936, but Jesse would have probably been an All-American.

8-3 "Chic" Harley, 1919, winning 13-3, with a TD run and four interceptions

8-4 Kicker John Kolesar

8-5 Four Times! Made for a "Hell of a Rivalry"

8-6 During Michigan Week, students and fans gather at Mirror Lake on campus on Thursday night and jump in. A Big Party!

8-7 Fritz Crisler (started at Princeton in 1935 but brought the concept to Michigan in 1938); Delaware also has a Blue & Yellow Winged Helmet

8-8 True. 5-4 against Notre Dame, 10-3 against Michigan State, but a losing record against the Buckeyes 6-7

8-9 Bob Ufer, long-time famed radio announcer at Michigan

8-10 Jim Laughlin, sending the #1 Ohio State Buckeyes to the Rose Bowl, winning 18-15

8-11 1934 Michigan game, Ohio State winning 34-0

8-12 Bo Schembechler, 2006. A standing ovation was given out of respect from the Ohio Stadium fans to honor the great Michigan coaching legend.

8-13 12-15-1, compared to Woody's record 16-11-1 (both in a 28-year span)

8-14 John Wilce

8-15 Tom Baldacci (Ohio State) and Lou Baldacci (Michigan). Ohio State won, 17-0, and the National Championship.

8-16 True. A common practice during the day, but Ohio State has never been accused of using "Tramp" players to win games.

8-17 Van Raaphorst; six in 1961

8-18 They both lost! #1 Ohio State to Illinois, 28-21, and Michigan to Wisconsin, 37-21

8-19 False: It was four out of five, split evenly. Bo 1972 & 1976; Woody 1973 & 1975.

8-20 6-7 career vs. Buckeyes; 1-6 against coach Jim Tressel

GROUP 9 QUESTIONS

9-1 Because the "10-Year War" between Bo and Woody was so dominant in the Big Ten, what was the conference called?

9-2 The year 2014 marked the 97th consecutive season for "The Game." Since 1897, and prior to "The Game" of 2014, which team led in victories?

9-3 What was Bo Schembechler's most famous quote?

9-4 Which year did #4 Michigan (10-0) outscore its opponents 235-48, while #1 Ohio State (10-0) had a scoring edge of 297-27 played to a tie?

9-5 **T or F:** Paul Brown, Ohio State Head Coach, was 1-1-1 against the Michigan Wolverines.

9-6 What four seasons did Ohio State BEAT Michigan by a combined score of 112-0?

9-7 Who threw three touchdown passes in the dedication game of the Michigan Stadium?

9-8 **T or F:** Coach Lloyd Carr won five of the first six games with Ohio State, then lost six of the next seven.

9-9 What was Fielding H. Yost's record against Ohio State, followed by Bo Schembechler's record?

9-10 **T or F:** Michigan was the first non-Ivy League team to win a National Title.

9-11 Which two Buckeye Head Coaches were Head Coaches at the famous Massillon Washington High School in Massillon, Ohio?

9-12 "Ace of Aces" in WWI, Eddie Rickenbacker grew up in the same neighborhood of what famous All-American Buckeye who was five years younger?

9-13 Name the fields Ohio State and Michigan played on the year before building their famous stadiums in the 1920s.

9-14 If the Heisman Trophy Award were given 20 years earlier, who might have been the first two-time winner?

9-15 During which game did Michigan fail to score with a first and goal on the Ohio State 1-yard line, for an undefeated season and a trip to the Rose Bowl?

9-16 Jim Otis scored four touchdowns in "The Game" in 1968, giving him 16 for the season. Whose record did he break?

9-17 **T or F:** During the BCS Era, the top two ranked teams have never played during the regular season.

9-18 Who was the first NCAA Division I FBS player to pass for 200 points and score 200 points?

9-19 Who did Fielding H. Yost call the Greatest Player of All-Time at Michigan?

9-20 Lame Duck Head Coach Earle Bruce was supported by his players in his final game against Michigan in 1997 through a display of what?

 GROUP 9 ANSWERS

9-1 "Big 2 and the Little 8"

9-2 (Michigan) 58-45-6

9-3 "Those who stay will be Champions" or some will say "The team-the team-the team"

9-4 1973, 10-10 Tie, Big Ten Conference Ads voted Ohio State to go to the Rose Bowl. Bo went ballistic, but this was the start for the Big Ten to play in more than just one bowl game.

9-5 True: He tied the first year (1941), won in 1942 (won Big Ten and National Championship); lost in 1943

9-6 Francis Schmidt-led teams of 1934-1937

9-7 Bennie Oosterbaan, future Head Football Coach at Michigan 1948-1958

9-8 True!

9-9 Yost 16-3-1; Bo 11-9-1

9-10 True! From 1901-1904, the Wolverines were 43-0-1 and outscored opponents 2,326 to 34.

9-11 Paul Brown and Earle Bruce

9-12 "Chic" Harley. Also, Archie Griffin and "Hopalong" Cassady grew up in Columbus, Ohio, a few years later.

9-13 Ohio State: Ohio Field; Michigan: Ferry Field

9-14 "Chic" Harley, Ohio State's first three time All-American; Red Grange of Illinois second

9-15 1972. Ohio State had a superb goal-line stand, led by Linebacker Rick Middletown.

9-16 Howard "Hopalong" Cassady

9-17 False! November 18, 2006: #1 OSU vs. #2 Michigan. Game titled as a "Game of the Century." Second one in the "Shoe;" Notre Dame was the first in 1935.

9-18 #7 Rick Leach, 1975-1978

9-19 Willie Heston

9-20 "EARLE" headbands; Earle beat Bo that day 23-20 on a Matt Frantz field goal.

GROUP 10 QUESTIONS

10-1 **T or F:** Ohio State has a Big Ten – Best 42 Conference Championships; Michigan is second with 34 Conference Championships.

10-2 Which three Big Ten coaches have had one or more 20-game winning streaks?

10-3 Which year was the first time the winner of "The Game" would be the outright Big Ten Champion?

10-4 Which two Ohio State players hold the record for the number of touchdowns and points in a Michigan game?

10-5 What does W.W. stand for in W.W. (Woody) Hayes' name?

10-6 What was Bo's record on Bowl games overall and in the Rose Bowl in particular?

10-7 Since 1929, when did both teams have first-year Head Coaches in "The Game?"

10-8 Which team in "The Game" was known as the "Mad Magicians?"

10-9 **T or F:** From 1968 through 1980 (13 seasons), the Big Ten Rose Bowl Representative was either Ohio State or Michigan.

10-10 What was the title of the movie telling the story of one of the great Big Ten Heisman Trophy winners?

10-11 Initially, what was the "Winged Helmet" designed to accomplish?

10-12 Who was the famous 1st drum major for The Ohio State University Marching Band?

10-13 Name the two Columbus, Ohio, Eastside High School football fields named after great Buckeye players in "The Game."

10-14 Which quarterback, in his final game against Michigan, threw for 330 yards and three touchdowns?

10-15 **T or F:** In the 2006 game, Michigan's defense was ranked #3 in the nation, allowing only 231.4 YPG and the best against the run at 29.9 YPG and had only given up three rushing TDs.

10-16 What does the number 99,391 represent?

10-17 Who said the following "Bulletin Board" material? "All Ohio football players don't go to Michigan, only the good ones."

10-18 What was the winning Pick 4 numbers in Ohio's Lottery, November 18, 2006?

10-19 Who was the second Ohio State Quarterback to BEAT Michigan three times in a row?

10-20 What was the record Coach Urban Meyer took into "The Game" of 2014 in regards to consecutive regular season Big Ten games?

GROUP **10** ANSWERS

10-1   False. Just the opposite. Michigan is the leader.

10-2   Fielding H. Yost, Michigan (2); Urban Meyer (3); Joe Paterno (2)

10-3   1944. Ohio State (18), Michigan (14). There were five lead changes, but Heisman Trophy Winner Les Horvath scored the winning touchdown.

10-4   24 points; four touchdowns by Bob Ferguson (1961), Jim Otis (1968)

10-5   Wayne Woodrow

10-6   Overall 5-12; 2-8 in the Rose Bowl

10-7   2011. Ohio State's Luke Fickell and Michigan's Brady Hoke, with Michigan winning 40-34.

10-8   1947 AP National Champion Michigan Wolverines for their complex shift, stunts and schemes.

10-9   True!

10-10   "Harmon of Michigan," 1941

10-11   To help the quarterback distinguish their receivers!

10-12   1920, Tubby Essington

10-13   Eastmoor High School (now Eastmoor Academy) has "Archie Griffin Field;" East High School has "Harley Field"

10-14   Joe Germaine, 1998

10-15   True! But Ohio State had 503 total yards and 187 by rushing and two rushing touchdowns.

10-16   Largest Spring Football Game attendance record, April 19, 2015. This will probably be broken again in the near future.

10-17   Michigan's QB Dennis Franklin, 1972. Michigan lost the game.

10-18   4 2 3 9. Same as the score: OSU 42, Michigan 39. Strange!

10-19   #10 QB Troy Smith, 2004-05-06; Tippy Dye

10-20   23 consecutive Big Ten wins; then he won "The Game," making the record 24 going into the 2015 season.

GROUP 11 QUESTIONS

11-1   "You'll never win a bigger game" referred to which Head Coach and which game?

11-2   How many yards did Tim Biakabutuka run for on 37 carries beating the 11-0, #2-ranked Ohio State Buckeyes 31-23? What year?

11-3   **T or F:** From 1972 to 1977, Woody Hayes' teams won or shared six Big Ten titles.

11-4   Which Head Coach called the trick play "Fumbleroski" in "The Game?"

11-5   **T or F:** Bo Schembechler played for Woody at Miami University and was twice an assistant coach at Ohio State. It is safe to say Bo's teams at Michigan were molded in the spirit of Woody Hayes' Ohio State teams.

11-6   Head Coach Urban Meyer set the record for all-time consecutive wins at what number?

11-7   What is the all-time record for Ohio State vs. Michigan as Big Ten members through 2014, including the vacated victory in 2010?

11-8   Which band in "The Game" was known as the "Transcontinental Band?"

11-9   Who is the only defensive player so far to win the Heisman Trophy?

11-10   Which Ohio State Heisman Trophy winner won with the widest margin?

11-11   **T or F:** Head Coach Earle Bruce only went undefeated once in the Big Ten Conference.

11-12   **T or F:** Historians state more people came to East High School in Columbus, Ohio to watch Chic Harley than Ohio State at the time.

11-13   What year did the Big Ten's ADs vote to send Ohio State to the Rose Bowl after a 10-10 tie with the undefeated Michigan Wolverines?

11-14   How many times has Ohio State been shutout in "The Game," through 2014?

11-15   How many points did Ohio State score in the fourth quarter when they BEAT Michigan 50-20 in 1961?

11-16   What four colors are on a Buckeye helmet?

11-17   Which year was "The Game" set to play after Thanksgiving because of the Big Ten Conference rescheduling?

11-18   In 1969, how many points did Ohio State average per game through the first eight games?

11-19   In Head Coach Jim Tressel's first victory against #11 Michigan in 2001, who ran for 129 yards and scored three touchdowns?

11-20   Who was the quarterback when Bob Ferguson scored four touchdowns against Michigan in 1961 and later became an assistant coach for Woody Hayes?

GROUP 11 ANSWERS

11-1 Bo Schembechler upsetting Woody's 1969 team; the start of the "Ten-Year War"

11-2 313 yards, in 1995

11-3 True! Five ties, one outright in 1975

11-4 Head Coach Earle Bruce, with Jim Lachey the pulling guard

11-5 Absolutely True: Run, Run, and Run some more. Running teams usually win the Big Ten.

11-6 24. In 2012-2013, he finally lost to Michigan State 34-24 in the Big Ten Championship Game.

11-7 46-46-4

11-8 Michigan, for playing in both Yankee Stadium and the Rose Bowl in 1950

11-9 1997 Michigan's Charles Woodson; 18 career interceptions in a three-year span

11-10 Troy Smith 2006, 91.6% of the first-place votes

11-11 True; went 8-0 in Big Ten League play, lost the Rose Bowl by one point and the National Championship, ending up 11-1 for the season in 1979.

11-12 True!

11-13 1973

11-14 27 times; last time 1993; Michigan has been shutout only 11 times

11-15 29 points!

11-16 Silver helmet with scarlet, white and black center strips. Decorated with Buckeye Award Leaves!

11-17 2009

11-18 46 points per game before losing to Michigan 24-12 in a major upset. Ohio State was a 17-point favorite.

11-19 Jonathan Wells

11-20 #25 Quarterback John Mummey

GROUP 12 QUESTIONS

12-1   **T or F:** Michigan was always unbeaten going into "The Game" from 1972 through 1975, and only beat the Buckeyes once.

12-2   Who stated: "To sense the intensity, the enthusiasm of a man destined to be a winner"?

12-3   How is the mispronunciation of Michigan spelled?

12-4   What position did Michigan Head Coach Gary Moeller play while co-captain at Ohio State under Coach Woody Hayes?

12-5   What has been the greatest margin of victory for the Ohio State Buckeyes in Ann Arbor?

12-6   Woody had 13 Big Ten Conference Championships; who is second with six?

12-7   Which arrogant, pompous Michigan Wolverine was smoking a victory cigar in front of his Coach Fritz Crisler on the sidelines when beating Ohio State in 1939?

12-8   How many Big Ten Championships and National Championships did Michigan Head Coach Lloyd Carr win?

12-9   **T or F:** Head Coach Earle Bruce had six straight years with a 9-3 season record.

12-10 What was the first year great Buckeye and Wolverine players could play varsity football as freshmen?

12-11 When is Bo Schembechler's birthday?

12-12 What was the worst "homer" call against Woody Hayes' Buckeyes, which resulted in a 15-yard penalty for "unsportsmanlike conduct" for Woody?

12-13 Who coached Michigan to two upset victories that ruined the National Championship Title hopes for the Buckeye teams ranked #2 in the country at the time of "The Game?"

12-14 Which Coach was the first to BEAT Michigan (1919) and first win in the "Horseshoe" in 1922?

12-15 **T or F:** Michigan held Archie Griffin to 46 rushing yards to snap his string of 31 straight 100-plus yards rushing per game.

12-16 What did the 1970 win (20-9) over Michigan mean for the senior class of Buckeyes who were dubbed the "Super Sophomores?"

12-17 "Carmen Ohio," Ohio State's Alma Mater, was written on a train after which loss to Michigan?

12-18 Which two #2-ranked teams did Ohio State beat in 2006?

12-19 Which son and brother of two Buckeye Heisman Trophy winners made interceptions to break a tie (14 all) to win 21-14 in 1975?

12-20 Which Ohio State Head Coach played at Michigan?

 GROUP **12** ANSWERS

12-1   False. They tied 10-10 in 1973.

12-2   AD Don Canham, during the 15-minute interview to hire Bo Schembechler as Michigan's 15th Head Coach.

12-3   "Meeechegan," as spoken by Head Coach Fielding H. Yost. Meeechegan™ is a registered trade name of the author.

12-4   Linebacker and Co-Captain 1961-1963

12-5   1935; 38 points by Head Coach Francis Schmidt

12-6   Jim Tressel. A seventh one, 2010, was vacated.

12-7   Forest "Evy" Evashevski, lead blocker for Tom Harmon and future Iowa Hawkeye Head Coach.

12-8   Five Big Ten Championships and the 1997 National Championship

12-9   True. 1980-1985; went 4-2 during this period in Bowl Games

12-10 1972; "Welcome Archie Griffin"

12-11 April Fool's Day (April 1, 1929); Woody's birthday is Valentine's Day (February 14, 1913)

12-12 1971; Michigan's Darden over the back pass interference on Ohio State's Dick Wakefield

12-13 Lloyd Carr

12-14 John Wilce, who also coached first three-time All-American "Chic" Harley

12-15 True, but Ohio State won the game 21-14 in 1975

12-16 They never lost a game in the "Horseshoe"

12-17 1902; 86-0 loss. Written by Fred Cornell and now sung after each home game; this tradition was started by Jim Tressel.

12-18 Michigan and the University of Texas

12-19 1975, Craig Cassady, son of "Hopalong" Cassady; Ray Griffin, Archie's younger brother

12-20 A.E. Herrnstein, 1906-1909, with a 28-10-1 record at Ohio State, 0-4 against Michigan

GROUP 13 QUESTIONS

13-1   What was Head Coach Jim Tressel's win/lose record against the Michigan Wolverines between 2004 and 2010?

13-2   LB Chris Spielman set the standard for the number of tackles in one game, which happened to be a Michigan game, at what number?

13-3   What year was #2 Ohio State upset 13-9 when BD Shawn Springs slipped, and Tai Streets caught a long touchdown pass for the Wolverines?

13-4   **T or F:** In the "Snow Bowl," Michigan did not make a first down, nor did they complete a pass on nine attempts.

13-5   What was Head Coach Wes Fesler's record against the Michigan Wolverines?

13-6   **T or F:** Woody won the 1952 Michigan game, which was the first OSU victory in eight years.

13-7   What year was the first time the "Gold Pants" were awarded to Buckeyes for beating Michigan?

13-8   T or F: Woody and Bo were both compatriots of what famous coaching group not in the Big Ten Conference?

13-9   **T or F:** Through 2014, Michigan has interrupted five unbeaten seasons for the Buckeyes. Ohio State has handed Michigan their first loss of a season six times.

13-10   Which Head Coach in "The Game" is known as "The Father of Two-Platoon Football?"

13-11   Which former player started the "Tunnel of Pride" before "The Game" in 1994, a tradition that has repeated ever since?

13-12   Who was the first Buckeye Coach to have a winning career record against Michigan?

13-13   Bo Schembechler was followed by two of his assistants, who became Wolverine Head Coaches. Who were they, and how many wins and losses did they have against Ohio State overall?

13-14   **T or F:** The "Super Sophomores" went 27-2 from 1968–1970, and Archie Griffin's teams went 40-5-1 from 1972–1975.

13-15   Head Coach Wes Fesler's last game was when, and against whom?

13-16   2006, Final Standing: Michigan trailed Florida by how many points in the BCS Rankings, which prevented a rematch with the Buckeyes for the National Championship?

13-17   Composer John Phillip Sousa called what song "College's Best Fight Song"?

13-18   How many times during the Ohio State vs. Michigan rivalry have both teams had a losing season?

13-19   Who lived in the White House the last time (before 2006) the Buckeyes beat a top-five ranked Michigan team?

13-20   What makes Buckeye nuts poisonous to humans, horses and cattle?

GROUP **13** ANSWERS

13-1   7 victories straight, last one vacated.

13-2   29, 1986 Michigan Game

13-3   1996. Buckeyes went on to win the Rose Bowl, but ended up the season ranked #2.

13-4   True! And they punted 24 times for 723 yards but won (upset) the Buckeyes 9-3.

13-5   Three losses and one tie; never BEAT Michigan from 1947-1950

13-6   True! Lost in 1953, and the fans started to call for Woody's head.

13-7   1934, Coach Francis Schmidt's motivating comment, beating Michigan 34-0

13-8   "Cradle of Coaches" at Miami University, along with numerous other Head Football Coaches of notable fame.

13-9   True

13-10   Fritz Crisler, Head Coach at Michigan, 1938-1947

13-11   #10 Rex Kern, Quarterback of the 1968 National Champions

13-12   Francis Schmidt (1934-1940), with a record of 4-3-0

13-13   1969-2007, Gary Moeller 3-1-1 and Lloyd Carr 6-7-0, for a total 9-8-1

13-14   True, beating Michigan six out of the seven games

13-15   1950, Michigan in the "Snow Bowl." His record was 0-3-1 vs. Michigan.

13-16   0.0101 points! Both Ohio State and Michigan lost their Bowl Games.

13-17   "The Victors," the University of Michigan

13-18   Once in 1959, Ohio State 3-5-1 and Michigan 4-5

13-19   President Gerald Ford, a Michigan center and MVP

13-20   Tannic acid

 GROUP **14** QUESTIONS

14-1   **T or F:** From 1897 through 1927, Michigan had a winning record of 19-3-2 against the Ohio State Buckeyes.

14-2   How many undefeated teams did Bo Schembechler have in 21 seasons at Michigan?

14-3   Name the two College Football Hall of Fame players who became Head Coaches at Michigan and who coached against Woody Hayes.

14-4   Which Wolverine Head Coach won an Associated Press (AP) National Championship and Coach of the Year honors in his first year?

14-5   **T or F:** None of the newspaper articles about Michigan beating Michigan State mentioned the introduction of Michigan's "NEW" Winged Helmet.

14-6   Who was the first Michigan Head Coach who could use the forward pass as a legal play?

14-7   When was the first All-American team? Who was the first Buckeye and who was the first Wolverine to receive this honor?

14-8   Who stated: "I always mind losing to Ohio State, but I didn't mind so much today."?

14-9   Who wrote the following about which Buckeye: "If you never saw him with a football, we can't describe it to you, it wasn't like Red Grange or Tom Harmon or anybody else. It was kind of a cross between music and cannon fire and it brought your heart up under your ears."?

14-10   Who said: "He's a better young man than he is a football player, and he's the best football player I've ever seen."?

14-11   In which Michigan game did underdog Ohio State lose the stats game (Michigan's 344 yards to OSU's 192) and the number of plays (83 to 44), but won the game and a Rose Bowl trip?

14-12   Which Buckeye Heisman Trophy winner epitomized the "Triple-Threat" football player?

14-13   Which Nickelback intercepted UM QB John Navarre's pass to Braylon Edwards to ensure a victory (14-9) in 2002 and a trip to the Fiesta Bowl National Championship game?

14-14   The 235-member Michigan Marching Band has what for its trademark formation?

14-15   In the 1960s, which Ohio State vs. Michigan game was delayed for a week?

14-16   What year did the Buckeyes tear down the "M CLUB SUPPORTS YOU" banner in Ann Arbor?

14-17   Who was the first and only Buckeye QB to throw four touchdown passes (so far) in "The Game?"

14-18   What year did Ohio State BEAT Michigan, breaking their string of 21 straight home wins?

14-19   The worst snow storm since 1913 swept into Columbus for the great "Snow Bowl" game in 1950. How many official inches of snow fell?

14-20   Who has the longest punt return for Michigan against Ohio State?

GROUP **14** ANSWERS

14-1 True, but since the Modern Era, 1950 and beyond, it is a different story.

14-2 None

14-3 Bennie Oosterbaan (1948-1958) and Bump Elliott (1959-1968)

14-4 Bennie Oosterbaan, 1948

14-5 True; no real interest in the helmet at this time

14-6 Fielding H. Yost, 1906. Helped with lowering injuries from the "Mass Wedge" plays; 18 deaths in 1905.

14-7 1898. Started by Walter Camp. Buckeyes' first All-American was "Chic" Harley; Michigan's first All-American was Willie Heston, selected by Walter Camp.

14-8 Bo Schembechler to Earle Bruce after Ohio State BEAT Michigan 1987, after Earle was fired earlier that week.

14-9 Schoolmate, Humorist and Writer James Thurber, writing about "Chic" Harley

14-10 Ohio State Head Football Coach Woody Hayes, speaking of Archie Griffin

14-11 The 1972 Game, and this was Archie's first trip to four straight Rose Bowls.

14-12 Vic Janowicz: A running back who also passed, punted, was a placekicker, played defense and was a very good blocker.

14-13 Will Allen

14-14 A Big Capital Block "M"

14-15 1963, because of the JFK assassination

14-16 1973, the 10-10 "Tie Game"

14-17 #19 QB Troy Smith, 2006

14-18 November 22, 1975; 21-14 on a Ray Griffin game-winning interception

14-19 Officially nine inches, with more snow forecast to come on Sunday

14-20 Desmond Howard, 93 yards, 1991; Heisman Trophy winner that year

GROUP **15** QUESTIONS

15-1   What year did the regular-season-ending game become "The Game" against the University of Michigan Wolverines?

15-2   What year was the "payback" game in the Rivalry?

15-3   With a 96-16-3 record during the 1970s, who was the best of any Division I Coaches?

15-4   Who are the two Michigan Wolverines to earn three-time All-American honors?

15-5   Who stated: "If you are going to play football, why don't you put on a suit?"

15-6   Which Ohio State Head Coach was fired during "BEAT MICHIGAN WEEK" but went on to upset the Wolverines in Ann Arbor 23-20?

15-7   Who were Lloyd Carr's two Major Award-winning players?

15-8   **T or F:** After Michigan won the 1943 Big Ten Championship (8-1) but lost to Notre Dame, ND would not schedule Michigan again for 30 years.

15-9   Which Michigan Head Football Coach stated about Woody Hayes: "I have a deep, abiding respect and admiration … He is one of the greatest coaches who ever coached the game."?

15-10 Who was known for his wide-open "Razzle-Dazzle" style of play and BEAT Michigan his first four years as Head Coach at Ohio State?

15-11 **T or F:** The wolverine is not a native animal of the state of Michigan.

15-12 Which team has the most All-Americans, most individuals and most two-time and three-time winners?

15-13 When Ohio State first played Michigan in 1897, how many points for a TD and how many points for the conversion?

15-14 What was U of M Coach Bo Schembechler's Rose Bowl record after playing against Woody?

15-15 Which two-time Buckeye All-American blocked Michigan punts in two consecutive games?

15-16 About which Michigan game did Woody Hayes state: "Our greatest comeback and the greatest game I've ever coached."?

15-17 Who won two National Championships, one at Ohio State in 1942 and the second one after WWII at Michigan in 1947?

15-18 Michigan Avenue in Columbus, Ohio, is temporarily named what during BEAT Michigan Week?

15-19 Since 1935, how many times has the Big Ten football championships been decided by the Ohio State–Michigan game?

15-20 **T or F:** The Home Depot's number-one selling Collegiate Paint Scheme in its team colors program is Ohio State's Scarlet and Gray.

GROUP **15** ANSWERS

15-1 1935

15-2 1970; Ohio State 21, Michigan 7, for the previous year upset loss 24-12 in Ann Arbor

15-3 Bo Schembechler at Michigan

15-4 Bennie Oosterbaan and Anthony Carter

15-5 Amos Alonzo Stagg, after knocking over Fritz Crisler upon meeting each other at a practice session at the University of Chicago.

15-6 Head Coach Earle Bruce

15-7 Charles Woodson, Heisman Trophy Winner 1997; LaMarr Woodley, 2006

15-8 False. It was Michigan who would not schedule Notre Dame.

15-9 Michigan Head Coach Jim Harbaugh

15-10 Francis Schmidt, 1934-1940

15-11 True! Not a verifiable trapping in the whole state of Michigan

15-12 Ohio State

15-13 Four points for a TD; two points for a conversion. Final score: 34-0

15-14 0-5

15-15 Iolas Huffman, 1920-1921

15-16 1975 in Ann Arbor; #1 Buckeyes won 21-14

15-17 J.T. White

15-18 Buckeye Way

15-19 23 Times

15-20 True! Michigan is third; Notre Dame is fifth

Numerology

0. Shutout: The goal of all defensive teams!

1. #1 Braxton Edwards WR Michigan All-American: three consecutive years receiving over 1,000 yards

   #1: The goal of both teams to be first in the Big Ten, then #1 National Champions

   A 1-point loss by the 1979 Buckeyes in the Rose Bowl cost them a National Championship for Coach Earle Bruce

2. 2! is the total number of wins Coach John Cooper had against Michigan in 13 games

   In 19(02), Michigan played its first college football Bowl Game, the Rose Bowl

3. 3 points for a field goal; missed and made ones have both cost Ohio State and the Wolverines games and winning championships

   Michigan has 3 Heisman Trophy winners

   20(03): 100th game, Michigan winning 35-21

4. #4 QB Jim Harbaugh's college number; won the Head Coaching job at Michigan going into the 2015 season

5. Woody's five National Championships (1954, 1957, 1961, 1968 and 1970)

6. Ohio State has 6 perfect seasons, no losses or ties through 2014

   6 National Championships won by Michigan Coach Fielding H. Yost

7. #7 Rick Leach, Michigan QB, All-American in both football and baseball, beat the Buckeyes three years in a row: 1976-77-78

   Ohio State has had 7 Heisman Trophy winners through 2014

   20(07): Michigan BEAT by Appalachian State Mountaineers!

8. Ohio State has won 8 National Championships going into the 2015 season

   Michigan has 8 alumni in the Pro Football Hall of Fame

9. 9 former Ohio State players and/or coaches are in the Pro Football Hall of Fame

   2016 Big Ten Conference to play a 9-game conference schedule

   Jim Nein, #9, first to win a Buckeye Leaf in 1967

10. #10 QB Troy Smith (Heisman Trophy winner 2006); #10 QB Rex Kern (National Champion 1968)

    The "Ten-Year War," Woody Hayes vs. Bo Schembechler, 1969-1978

 **Numerology**

11. Retired number at Michigan for all three Wistert brothers, Francis, Albert and Alvin; all three brothers All-American tackles

    11 National Championships for Michigan through 2014

    11 All-Americans played on the 1968 Ohio State National Championship Team

    20(11): Michigan's first night game in Michigan Stadium

12. 20(12): Michigan wins 900th program win against Michigan State

    12 points scored by the #1 Buckeyes when upset by Bo and the Wolverines in 1969, 24-12

    12-0: Urban Meyer's first-year record at Ohio State, 2012

13. 13-13 tie with Michigan (1992), saved John Cooper's job by President Gordon Gee

    19(13): Ohio State wins Big Ten Conference

    Bo won 13 Big Ten Titles

14. 20(14) National Championship, beating Oregon 42-20 in first BCS Championship game series

15. It took a 15-minute interview by AD Don Canham to hire Bo Schembechler in 1969

16. Number of times Woody BEAT Michigan in his 28 years at Ohio State

    19(16): First year Ohio State won a Big Ten Championship

17. Ohio State was undefeated, had a 22-game winning streak, and was a 17-point favorite, but was upset by Bo 24-12 in 1969, starting the "Ten-Year War"

18. 19(18): Michigan won first Big Ten Conference game against the Buckeyes, 14-0, at Ohio Field

    19(18): Michigan won the Big Ten 2-0 (5-0) with a dispute from Illinois who was 4-0 in the Big Ten and 5-2 overall

    #18 QB Craig Krenzel, 14-0 National Champion, beating Miami 31-24 in double overtime

19. 19(19): Ohio State BEAT Michigan for the first time 13-3; led by "Chic" Harley

20. Jim Harbaugh, hired December 14, 2014, is Michigan's 20th Head Football Coach

21. 21: the number of All-Americans recruited by John Cooper at Ohio State!

    Bo Schembechler coached 21 seasons at Michigan, 1969-1989

    #21 Punter B.J. Sander won the Ray Guy Award in 2003; against Michigan, he averaged 49.1 yards per punt on nine punts

 # Numerology

22. #22 Les Horvath, Heisman Trophy winner 1944, led Ohio State to their first National Championship in 1942

    19(22): Ohio Stadium built

    22 veteran players leave for WWII in 1942

    22-game winning streak that Woody took into the 1969 Michigan game

23. #23 "Arnie" Chonko, All-American in Football and Baseball at Ohio State

    Michigan was 8-0-0 in 19(23) but lost Big Ten Conference to Illinois, who was also 8-0-0, but they were 5-0 in conference to Michigan's 4-0 record; both beat Ohio State

24. 24 straight victories by Coach Urban Meyer, BEATING Michigan 42-41 in Ann Arbor 2013

    24 Head Football Coaches at Ohio State in 121-year history

25. 19(25): Ohio loses fourth straight game to Michigan

    #25 Esco "Sark" Sarkkinen, All-American End and Assistant Coach at Ohio State from 1946 to 1978; known at the time as one of the best scouts in the college game

26. 19(26): First and only one-point victory for Michigan against the Buckeyes

    19(26): Maudine Ormsby, a cow, was named Homecoming Queen at Ohio State

27. #27 RB Eddie George, Heisman Trophy winner 1997; Big Ten MVP, Doak Walker and Maxwell Award winner

    19(27): Michigan Stadium built and designed after the Yale Bowl

28. 28 players involved in "Tattoogate," which resulted in Jim Tressel retiring

    19(28): First year for "The Ramp" entrance

29. 19(29): Coach Sam Willaman's first season; he BEAT Michigan 7-0; Michigan also had a first-year Coach, Happy Kipke; didn't happen again until 2011 (Luke Fickell vs. Brady Hoke)

30. Through 2014, 30 former Ohio State players and coaches have been inducted into the College Football Hall of Fame

31. #31 Vic Janowicz, Heisman Trophy winner 1950; often called the best athletic ever at Ohio State and labeled a true "Triple-Threat Player" because he could do it all!

32. #32 DB Jack Tatum, "The Assassin," fiercest defender, two-time All-American, National Champion 1968

33. #33 James Laurinaitis, three-time All-American, winner of the Nagurski Award 2006, Butkus Award 2007, and 2007 Big Ten Defensive Player of the Year

 # Numerology

34. Losing score in first game against Michigan was 34-0 in 1897 in Ann Arbor

    19(34): Year the "Gold Pants Charm," Captain's Breakfast, and Buckeye Grove began

    Ohio State players have won 34 major listed awards

    Ohio State players had 34 All-Americans in the 1970s

35. 19(35): Final game of the season to be "The Game;" also known as "Michigan Week"

36. #36 LB Chris Spielman, Ohio State, 546 career tackles, 283 solo tackles, two-time All-American, Lombardi Trophy winner

    #36 LB Tom Cousineau, two-time All-American, 211 tackles in 1978 (still a record), 16 solo against SMU in 1978

    19(36): Script Ohio played for the first time in the Horseshoe

37. Ohio State: 37 Conference Championships, including 35 Big Ten Titles and three Division Championships through 2014

    Since the 1936 AP Poll, Michigan has finished in the Top Ten 37 times

38. 19(38): The "Official Cheering Section" for the Buckeyes formed the "Block O"

    First year Michigan wore winged helmet under coach Fritz Crisler

    Tom Harmon & Paul Kromer known as the "Touchdown Twins" for Michigan

39. 19(39): Unranked Michigan beat #6 Ohio State 21-14 with 50 seconds left on the clock, but Ohio State still won the Big Ten Title; first one since 1920

    19(39): Dickinson Ranking System introduced, and Michigan ended up #7

    19(39): Michigan's Tom Harmon was second to Iowa's Nile Kinnick in Heisman Trophy Award

40. #40, RB Howard "Hopalong" Cassady, Heisman Trophy winner 1955; two-time All-American, 4,403 all-purpose yards

    19(40): Michigan's #98 Tom Harmon wins the Heisman Trophy Award

41. 19(41): QB Don Scott, two-time All-American, was killed while training in his B-26 in England; Ohio State Airport named "Don Scott Field"

    #41 FB Matt Snell carried the ball 30 times for 121 in Super Bowl, winning with Joe Namath for the first time for an AFL team. Matt was also a member of the greatest backfield Woody ever had with #42 Paul Warfield ("Lightning") and #46 Bob Ferguson ("Thunder"), both All-Americans and winners of numerous other awards

    19(41): Both Ohio State and Michigan ranked in the AP Poll's Top 25 for the first time

Numerology

42. Buckeyes scored 42 points against Michigan in 2006 to win 42-39 in the "Game of the Century," #1 vs. #2

    19(42): First National Championship won under Coach Paul Brown

    42 league titles won or shared by Michigan through 2014

    #42 RB Paul Warfield, Pro Football Hall of Fame member, flipped the coin for the 2006 "Game of the Century" for "The Game"

    Ohio State holds the record for 42 touchdown passes in a season through 2014

43. 19(43) Michigan team received "Wisconsin's gold-plated gift" in the form of Elroy "Crazy Legs" Hirsch through the V-12 Navy College Training Program

    19(43): Michigan's victory over Ohio State (45-7) was the largest margin since the 86-0 win in 1902

    Heisman Trophy Winner Tom Harmon's wartime exploits included crashing in Brazil and shooting down Japanese Zeros in Hong Kong and Jiujiang, China

44. 44 yards is the longest TD pass in Big Ten Championship Game

    19(44): #3 Ohio State BEAT #6 Michigan 18-14 to win the Big Ten Championship with a perfect record; then the Buckeyes finished #2 nationally behind #1 Army; #1 all-civilian college team

45. #45 RB Archie Griffin, the one and only two-time Heisman Trophy winner 1974-1975, Big Ten MVP 1973-1974, College Football Hall of Fame

    19(45): Michigan coach Fritz Crisler introduces "two-platoon football"

46. 19(46): Former Coach Paul Brown becomes first coach and part-time owner of the Cleveland Browns

    #46 FB Bob Ferguson, two-time All-American, Maxwell winner, UPI College Player of the Year, second in Heisman Trophy voting by 56 points to Ernie Davis; never was tackled for a loss at Ohio State!

    #46 DB Ted Provost "The Tree," nicknamed by Woody Hayes for all the Buckeye Leaves he earned on his helmet; 1968, All-American and National Champion while playing with Jack Tatum and coached by Lou Holtz

47. #47 Bennie Oosterbaan, Michigan's Greatest All-Time Athlete!

    #47 "Chic" Harley – absolutely one of Ohio State's All-Time Greatest Players – BEAT Michigan single handedly in 1919; College Football Hall of Fame, three-time All-American, 21-1-1 college career

    #47 LB A.J. Hawk, All-American and Lombardi Trophy winner 2005

    19(47): Michigan team known as "Mad Magicians" for the high-power offense

    19(47): Bennie Oosterbaan wins National Championship

 **Numerology**

48. #48 Center Gerald Ford, Michigan MVP and later President of the United States

    19(48): Michigan team, undefeated 9-0-0 and Big Ten Conference Champion

49. 19(49): Buckeyes share the Big Ten 7-1-2 for Wes Fesler and win their first Rose Bowl

50. "Fifty Greatest Spirit Figures at Michigan" published by Sports Illustrated in 1999, includes: Oosterbaan, Kramer, Yost, Leach, Kipke and Ford

51. 51-42-2: Career record at Michigan for "Bump" Elliott, 1959-1968; 3-7 against the Buckeyes

52. 19(52): Woody Hayes BEATS heavily favored Michigan 27-7 for the first Ohio State victory over Michigan since 1944

53. #53 LB Randy Gradisher, two-time All-American, 1973 defense, recorded four shutouts and allowed just 64 points, but ... (see #64)

54. The 2,420-pound bell in the Horseshoe's Southeast Tower was rung for victories starting in 19(54); 15 minutes for a victory; 30 minutes for a victory over Michigan

55. 19(55): #40 HB Howard "Hopalong" Cassady wins the Heisman Trophy by the largest margin at the time, along with the Maxwell Trophy and the AP Athlete of the Year

56. Fielding H. Yost won 56 games in a row with his "Point-a-Minute" teams in early 1901-1905

    #56 LaMarr Woodley, Michigan's All-American and Lombardi Trophy winner 2006

57. 19(57): Woody's National Championship team lost its opener to TCU 18-14 but BEAT Michigan 31-14

58. 58 is the number of All-Americans who played for Woody Hayes at Ohio State

59. Bob Ufer, Michigan's famous radio announcer, was 59 when he described the famous Anthony Carter catch to beat Indiana with six seconds left in the game

60. 19(60): FB Bob Ferguson scores only touchdown in game, giving Ohio State a 7-0 victory; Woody became 6-4 against Michigan in first 10 years

61. 19(61): Football Writers' National Champion 8-0-1 Ohio State, OSU's 4th, Woody's 3rd BEAT Michigan 50-20 that year

62. #62 Guard Jim Parker, two-time All-American 1955-56, and Outland Trophy winner

63. 19(63): Michigan game delayed a week because of the JFK assassination

    63.4% Troy Smith's career passing completion percentage

Numerology

64. 64: The total number of points allowed by the 1973 Ohio State defense with four shutouts; but Michigan beat the Buckeyes 22-0! OUCH!

    19(64) Michigan 9-1 wins Big Ten Championship for the first time since 1950

65. In 19(65), "Hang on Sloopy" becomes Buckeye favorite song played at the start of the fourth quarter with O–H–I–O chant

66. 19(66): Woody's worst year, 4-5 overall, 3-4 in the Big Ten, in his 16th year

    66,210: original seating capacity in the Horseshoe in 1922

67. 19(67): Ohio State team lost first three games at home but BEAT Michigan 24-14

68. #68 LB Jim Stillwagon, Outland Trophy 1970, Lombardi Award 1970, UPI Lineman of the Year 1970, College Football Hall of Fame, two-time All-American

69. 19(69): first year for Bo Schembechler at Michigan and winning the upset of the "Greatest College Football Team Ever Assembled" 24-12, starting the "Ten-Year War"

70. 19(70) was a really crazy year, with Ohio State and Michigan alternating the ranking of #4 and #5. Michigan was #4 going into the game and favored to stay undefeated and win a trip to the Rose Bowl. Ohio State BEAT Michigan, 20-9, in what Woody Hayes called "the greatest defensive game that our team had ever had"

    #70 Tackle Dave Foley, All-American, National Champion 1968 and three-time Academic All-American

71. 19(71): Another classic game in the "Ten-Year-War," with Ohio State having a so-so year (6-3), and Michigan undefeated again. Michigan won this game 10-7, but it had "the worst called play in the history of college football," with an interference call that was NOT called — sending Woody ballistic! This just kept building "The Game" into the Greatest Rivalry in College Football!

72. All-Time winning percentage: .720 (863-319-53) through the 2014 season for Ohio State; Michigan has a .729 (915-328-36) winning percentage

    72,000 was the initial capacity in Michigan Stadium, built in 1927; today: 109,901

73. 19(73): Ohio State and Michigan tie 10-10, but the ADs vote to send the Buckeyes to the Rose Bowl. This makes BO ballistic, like Woody in 1971! After this, the Big Ten started to accept invitations to other Bowl Games besides just the Rose Bowl.

74. #74 Tackle John Hicks, first player from Ohio State to play in three Rose Bowls; runner-up in the 1973 Heisman Trophy voting, two-time All-American, Lombardi Trophy winner and Outland Trophy winner

 **Numerology**

75. #75 LT Orlando Pace: two-time All-American and first sophomore to win the Lombardi Trophy, 1995 and 1996

    19(75): Michigan starts a record string of home attendance of 100,000-plus that is still going strong into the 2015 season, which should see a new all-time record for "The Game"

76. Winning percentage of .761 for Woody Hayes (205-58-10)

    19(76): FB Pete Johnson sets career record for touchdowns with 56; several against the Wolverines in "The Game"

77. 19(77): #5 Michigan beats #4 Ohio State 14-6 in another "classic," continuing to build "The Game" to a level not matched by any other rivalry

78. The Michigan Wolverines have had 78 consensus All-Americans through 2014

    19(78): Woody fired after Gator Bowl loss, ending the "Ten-Year War"

79. 18(79): First year the Michigan Wolverines played football

80. 19(80): Bo Schembechler wins his first Rose Bowl, beating Washington 23-6

81. 18(81): Michigan plays Harvard in the first intersectional football game

82. 19(82): Michigan wins Big Ten Championship with second three-time All-American Anthony Carter

83. #83 Buckeye WR Terry Glenn: 1995 Biletnikoff Award winner, All-American

    Since 1983, visiting team wears white jerseys

84. #84 End Jim Houston: 1957-59, two-time All-American, two-time Buckeye MVP, leading receiver and Captain 1959

    #84 Defensive End Bob Brudzinski, All-American 1976, 4 interceptions as a DE!

85. 19(85): Michigan with new QB, #4 Jim Harbaugh (UM Head Coach 2015), played in another "Game of the Century," #2 vs. #1 Iowa, losing 12-10

    #85 Kicker Mike Nugent "Nooooge" wins 2004 Lou Groza Award

86. 1902: Michigan "thumps" Ohio State, 86-0!

87. #87 UM End, Ron Kramer, played both ways in 1955-56, winning All-American honors twice

    18(87): Michigan introduces football to students at Notre Dame

88. 19(88): Head Coach John Cooper's first season, with a 4-6-1 record, 2-5-1 in Big Ten play and lost to Michigan 34-31 on last-minute field goal

 # Numerology

89. 89 yards: longest run from scrimmage done by Dan "Boom" Herron against the Michigan Wolverines, 2010

90. 18(90): first football season for The Ohio State University Buckeyes

91. 19(91): Desmond Howard wins the Heisman Trophy; Michigan wins Big Ten Conference outright

92. 19(92): Ohio State and Michigan tie 13-13; OSU President Gordon Gee said: "This tie is one of our greatest wins ever!" Coach Cooper is now 0-4-1 in his first five years against Michigan, and QB (now ESPN football reporter) Kirk Herbstreit never did BEAT Michigan

93. 19(93): First of three years (along with 1995 & 1996) in which Ohio State was undefeated with National Championship aspirations, but lost all three Games to the Wolverines

94. 19(94): "Tunnel of Pride" began at the 1994 Michigan Game; created by Rex Kern, 1968 National Champion QB

95. 19(95): #2 Ohio State loses to Michigan 31-23, then loses to Tennessee 20-14 in the Citrus Bowl, after going 11-0 to start the season

96. 18(96): Michigan joins the Big Ten Conference in its inception

97. 19(97): Michigan claims its 11th National Championship with Head Coach Lloyd Carr and Heisman Trophy Winner Charles Woodson

98. "Old 98" Tom Harmon, Michigan's first Heisman Trophy winner, 1940

    18(98): "The Victors" written after Michigan beat the University of Chicago for first Western Conference Championship

99. #99 Bill Willis, Ohio State's UPI All-American, and one of the first two African-Americans to play pro football. He broke the color line a year before Jackie Robinson did in Major League Baseball; number retired and considered by many as the "best" to ever wear an Ohio State uniform

100. The 100th "Game" between the Ohio State Buckeyes and the Michigan Wolverines was in 2003; Michigan won 35-31

"THE GAME" Weather FORECAST
Weather Links for Ohio Stadium & Michigan Stadium

Ohio Stadium

http://forecast.weather.gov/MapClick.php?lon=-83.01977&lat=40.00160#.VdSzg_lVhBc

Latitude 40.0017 N; Longitude 83.0197 W; Elevation: 778 ft.

Michigan Stadium

http://forecast.weather.gov/MapClick.php?lon=-83.74872&lat=42.26587#.VdS0YPlVhBc

Latitude 42.2658 N; Longitude 83.7486 W; Elevation: 892 ft.

Additional Features
Radar & Satellite Images

Radar: http://radar.weather.gov/Conus/full.php

Satellite: http://www.weather.gov/satellite#ir

Hourly Weather Graphs

Hourly Weather Graphs include: Heat Index (F), Dew Point (F), Temperature (F), Gusts (mph), Surface Wind (mph), Relative Humidity (%), Precipitation Potential (%), Sky Cover (%), Rain, Thunder

Ohio Stadium Hourly Weather Graph

http://forecast.weather.gov/MapClick.php?site=ILN&&FcstType=graphical&cl=399889829874

Michigan Stadium Hourly Weather Graph

http://forecast.weather.gov/MapClick.php?lat=42.3177&lon=-83.7554&unit=0&lg=english&FcstType=graphical

Go Bucks!   Go Blue!